Commencement

Spiritual Journey

JADE BLAK

WESTBOW
PRESS
A DIVISION OF THOMAS NELSON
& ZONDERVAN

Copyright © 2015 Jade Blak.

All rights reserved. No part of this book may be used or reproduced by any means, graphic, electronic, or mechanical, including photocopying, recording, taping or by any information storage retrieval system without the written permission of the publisher except in the case of brief quotations embodied in critical articles and reviews.

Unless otherwise noted, all Scripture quotations are from the King James Version of the Bible.

WestBow Press books may be ordered through booksellers or by contacting:

WestBow Press
A Division of Thomas Nelson & Zondervan
1663 Liberty Drive
Bloomington, IN 47403
www.westbowpress.com
1 (866) 928-1240

Because of the dynamic nature of the Internet, any web addresses or links contained in this book may have changed since publication and may no longer be valid. The views expressed in this work are solely those of the author and do not necessarily reflect the views of the publisher, and the publisher hereby disclaims any responsibility for them.

Any people depicted in stock imagery provided by Thinkstock are models, and such images are being used for illustrative purposes only. Certain stock imagery © Thinkstock.

ISBN: 978-1-4908-6957-5 (sc)
ISBN: 978-1-4908-6958-2 (hc)
ISBN: 978-1-4908-6956-8 (e)

Library of Congress Control Number: 2015902279

Printed in the United States of America.

WestBow Press rev. date: 02/19/2015

Contents

Acknowledgments xi
Introduction xiii

Phase One: Broken 1
Chapter 1: The Journey Begins 3
Chapter 2: Suspect 15
Chapter 3: Missing Child 25
Chapter 4: A New Perspective 29

Phase Two: Shattered 33
Chapter 5: Facing Reality 35
Chapter 6: Starting Over 41

Phase Three: Mending the Pieces 45
Chapter 7: Seeking Change 47
Chapter 8: New Life 51

Phase Four: Closure 55
Chapter 9: Recommencement 57
Chapter 10: Transforming 67
Chapter 11: Testimony 77

Appendix 87

To my children, nieces, and nephews who did not have the opportunity to have a relationship with Kenya; my parents and my siblings, who were always there for me; and my husband, whose cooperation has been invaluable.

Epiphany 2008

In everything give thanks for this is the will of God concerning you. (1 Thess. 5:8)

Acknowledgments

I would like to thank my Uncle A. D., who suggested that I keep a journal; Uncle G. E., who on every visit reminded me that I needed to get this done; and Auntie B. J., who simply said it's time—may you rest in peace.

I would also like to thank my overseer D.G.P., and elect lady M.M.P., who did not compromise God's Word, which helped me to discover the truth and understand that God will establish me and man must live by every word that proceeds from the mouth of God.

Finally, I would like to thank Mr. William Llewellyn, who gave me the insight to complete this project; and Mr. Miguel Duarte, who helped me officially put this book together.

Introduction

I was living in the Deep South, where the temperature was 90 degrees with a heat index of 100 and it was very humid, the kind of weather that made you feel sticky if you were exposed for a long length of time. I was living in a single-wide mobile home; the surrounding trees were the only thing that could eliminate the sting of the heat beaming on the aluminum frame as the air-conditioning continued running to cool the inside. One Friday evening, my three-year-old son was picked up to go out of town with my in-laws, who enjoyed spending time with him; my six-year-old daughter had been picked up by her paternal grandmother, who lived here in town. My thoughts were, *Yeah, I have no children for the weekend.* Who would have ever thought that this would be the worst weekend of my life?

PART ONE

Broken

CHAPTER 1

The Journey Begins

Through the journey of life, we grow in our experience and understanding of the world and try to comprehend our place in it. Yet in spite of what we learn, one thing is certain: we all believe in something. Though I always had religion, I now realize that the lack of increased knowledge led me astray, but I never forgot that there is a higher being. My family taught me to have faith, follow the commandments of God, repent of my sins in order to be forgiven, and know that God loves me, no matter what. From this basis of understanding, I thought I was ready for the world. But there was something more I had to learn. My first challenge came in a dream.

At our family home, Big Mama was sitting at the table drinking her Sanka and enjoying her Kool 100s. Other family members were present and seemed to be preparing to go somewhere. The front door was open, and I saw blue skies and sunshine.

I also saw a white limousine parked in front of the house, and I thought to myself, *Why?*

One by one the family members were going into a church, and I too was in this line. I saw my mother's siblings, but I did not see her. I saw my father's siblings, but I did not see him. As I approached the pulpit, a white casket was in place of the communion table. With my heart racing and my breathing labored, I immediately awakened before viewing the body.

I then realized it was only a dream, though it had seemed so real. I was filled with dread, frightened that I was about to lose one of my parents. I was very much afraid and did not want to tell anyone, but I couldn't keep it to myself.

I had been told about the spiritual gifts that many of my family members possessed, but I did not concern myself with them because I was more concerned with the things of the world. When I told my sister Tamika about my dream, she said, "Don't worry about it because you did not see anyone."

> And it shall come to pass in the last days, saith God, I will pour out My Spirit upon all flesh; and your sons and your daughters shall prophesy, and your young men shall see visions, and your old men shall dream dreams. (Acts 2:17)

Two weeks later, on Mother's Day weekend, as I was doing my Saturday morning ritual, I heard *ring, ring, ring, ring!* When I answered the telephone, it was Tamika, who invited me to her home in the country for a birthday barbeque for her husband, Marty. I told her that my husband, Kevin, a local grocery store manager, was at work, but when he got off, I would be glad to come. We didn't have the children that weekend, as they were at their paternal grandparents', and Kevin and I had a romantic time planned. Tamika asked if I could come sooner to help with the preparations, but I couldn't because Kevin and I only had one car and he had taken it to work. The conversation ended, and I proceeded to clean my house.

I started wiping the refrigerator door when, all of a sudden, a shiver came over me and the hairs on my arms stood up as if something were rising and leaving my body. I shook it off, hoping I was coming down with something, and continued to clean.

After I finished cleaning the kitchen, I sat down on the couch to take a break. Suddenly there was an urgent pounding on the front door. My heart stopped as my mind went back to the dream, wondering if something had happened to one of my parents. I nervously opened the door to find a female deputy sheriff standing there.

"Are you Nicole Dean?" she asked.

"Yes."

Handing me a piece of paper, she said, "You're to report to court."

"What for?" I asked.

She stated that the summons was for an increase in child support scheduled for the following week. I told her I was unaware that I would be going to court and asked if Mr. Derek Smith knew.

"Yes," she replied. "I've already been to his home. His wife received the information."

I smiled and thanked her, for this was an unexpected surprise. Derek and I were high school sweethearts and had a child together, our daughter Kenya, before graduating. Derek wanted to do the right thing and get married upon my graduating. However, I felt that I was too young and needed to figure out what I wanted to do in life before becoming a wife, so I turned him down and chose to no longer be in a relationship with him. That's when the relationship started drifting into resentment.

> The fear of the Lord is the beginning
> of knowledge: but fools despise wisdom
> and instruction. (Prov. 1:7)

Proceeding with my to-do list, I cleaned Kenya's room and thought about when I kissed her on the forehead the night before, after she had gone to sleep, looking so innocent. I reminisced about the day she was born. My parents' first grandchild, Kenya was born on my mother's birthday in Long Beach, California, a beautiful and healthy eight-pound, six-ounce baby girl. I could not believe she was mine. I thought back on how Derek, our friends, and I had skipped school to take me to get an abortion. I understood why Derek wanted to do this, but my heart was saddened, and I was just going along with it. However, upon arrival, they found I was too far along, and so they could not perform the procedure. I was so relieved. God knew my heart.

Once more I was interrupted by *ring, ring, ring, ring!* I answered to hear my mother's trembling voice shouting, "Bea," she began, "Kenya is missing!"

Horror-struck, I stood silent for a moment and then asked, "When? How could this be? Isn't she at her grandmother's house?" Sickened, my stomach turned.

My mother went on to explain the details she knew. Kenya's stepmother, Bessie, had called her in-laws and told them Kenya was missing and that she needed help looking for her. Bessie alleged she had scolded Kenya for wetting the bed. She said that Kenya had insisted she wanted to go back to her paternal grandmother's house—that's who I thought she was staying with, but plans had changed and her father had picked her up there the evening before. So Bessie told Kenya, "If you do, you can walk." Bessie put her three-year-old daughter down for a nap. Apparently Bessie too had fallen asleep and awakened to find Kenya gone.

I found it strange that no one had called me. I was stunned. Kenya knew my phone number. I could have gotten a ride to pick her up if she had wanted to come home. I asked my mother what Bessie had done.

"Like what?" she asked.

"Did Bessie contact the proper authorities?"

"I don't know, but I will find out and call you back."

I slammed down the telephone. I could not understand why Kenya's paternal family did not call me. As I pondered the situation, I was sure that Kenya would call me to let me know she was all right.

The more I thought about it, though, the angrier I became. This could not be; Kenya was afraid to be left alone. She would cry if we were separated at the grocery store. Feelings of fear burdened me. *What has happened to my child? What will I do if something has happened to her?*

I could not wait to hear what someone else had done in an attempt to find my child. I called the local police department to find that no one had called and that a person wasn't officially missing unless it had been forty-eight hours. This was before the Amber

Alert was implemented. I then contacted the local newspaper, the central Mississippi TV news, and the Missing Children Association to get the help I needed to find my baby while I was still waiting to hear from her father or stepmother.

When the word was out that a six-year-old girl was missing, all ethnic groups were concerned since this was the first time anything like this had ever happened in our town. Family members and friends started an immediate search for Kenya.

As I sat home waiting to hear from Kenya, it felt as if time had stopped. My mother periodically called to see if I had received any news and to inform me that Tamika would be coming soon in spite of her plans. She also informed me of the rally on campus led by Derek, a rally I had not been informed of.

Shortly after our conversation, there was a knock on the door. I opened it to find the county rescue squad. They wanted to inform me that they were assisting in the search and to reassure me that everything would be okay. I was grateful for their concern, and I thanked them as they were leaving the premises. Calls continued to flood the lines, but none were from Kenya. I did not want to seem rude when calls came in, but I did not want to tie up the line with long conversations since I hoped Kenya would contact me. I couldn't concentrate on anything else.

My mother called again, informing me that the Myers University detectives were handling the investigation because it happened on campus where Bessie and Derek lived. I was not pleased because I felt that if this was happening in my city, the city officials should be handling the situation. Sadly, all information obtained thus far was given by weekend parents that couldn't care less about my thoughts or concerns; I, on the other hand, was Kenya's mother.

The university detectives had taken a statement in particular from a gas station attendant, who stated a young lady came to the station to fill up her car. The young lady said she was on her way to Atlanta to pick up her husband. The attendant saw a little girl in the backseat and asked, "What is your name?" He understood her to say Kenya. How did he know to contact the university detectives if the child hadn't been declared missing in the city? Only by word of mouth would people have known, and like me, they would not have known the campus detectives were in charge of the investigation. Meanwhile at the rally downtown, I was being thrown under the bus by Derek because I was not present at the rally I was not informed of.

That same day shortly after dusk, my sister arrived and wanted an update on what was going on. I did not have much to say except, "Let's go find my baby," and "Take me to Derek's home, Pavilion Walk

Apartments, because I want to hear answers straight from the horse's mouth on what has happened." When we pulled up and stopped the car outside of Derek's apartment, two of his sisters were standing there. We kept the car running. Whatever happened at this point could have made the situation worse if I lost my composure. We calmly asked if they had heard anything. I was feeling so frustrated I wanted to jump out of the car and just start beating the daylights out of someone—as if that would return my child. Instead, I was praying to myself, "Lord keep me ...," as they told us no. Next I asked, "Where is your brother?" They replied, "He's not here, but his wife is in the house." Oh no, it was time to go; I did not want to give way to the devices of the enemy.

My sister wanted to bum-rush the wife, but I wanted to be home in case Kenya were trying to contact me. That's where I was going to be, so we headed back to my home. I knew that I was justified by the word of God because I had faith. The problem was I wasn't walking in the fullness of God's word. I was like many people: going to church out of tradition. I thanked God that I was reared in the church to learn the things that I understood about my beliefs. It gave me a foundation to lean on the word of God in my time of sorrow. For it is written: "Vengeance is mine; I will repay, saith the Lord." Romans 12:19

> Wisdom and knowledge shall be the stability of thy times, and strength of salvation: the fear of the LORD is his treasure. (Isa. 33:6)

After my sister dropped me off, she had to go back home to check on the guests there because the barbeque had not been canceled. That was okay because my husband was home from work at this time and I would not be alone.

At 9:00 p.m. there was a forceful knock at the door; I answered in hopes to finally have some answers. Chief Bubba Green, along with four additional campus detectives who were leading the investigation, were at my door in Pine Leaf Trailer Park to inform me that they were very concerned about my child being kidnapped. The officer asked if they could come in. I had answered the door hoping for some good news on Kenya's whereabouts. Instead, once in my home, the chief took me to the side and said, "You do know that it is a crime to make a false report?"

I replied "yes." But I was thinking *I was not even allowed to make a report.*

The chief then asked if he could search my home. I asked, "Why?"

Commencement

His reply was curt. "We have reason to believe that the missing child is here, and if we find her, you will be arrested."

I was outraged! Hesitant to speak, I finally stated I would not do something like that. I agreed to the search. It was completed from top to bottom, and there were no signs of Kenya. I felt violated after the search, as well as disgusted by their nerve. I was unaware of the things that were going on with this investigation and was not given the opportunity to make a report with the local police department.

"Casting all your care upon Him, for He cares for you." (1Peter 5:7)

CHAPTER 2

Suspect

Innocent until proven guilty is the creed of the law. Unfortunately, I was feeling very weary and drained, still in disbelief that this had happened to me: my firstborn was missing. I will always remember the birth of my firstborn. My cousin Deanne and I were in the mall when the contractions started. At first I thought it was just a quicken, another Braxton Hicks, so I just ignored it as nothing more. We continued to walk, and another, stronger quicken came. Little did I know that my cousin Deanne was timing them, and when the next intense pain hit, she said, "You are in labor." Mind you, the signs of labor that I had been taught had not occurred. There was no bloody show or fluids from the amniotic sac, yet I felt I should go to the hospital due to the pain. Instead, I was taken home. The doctor was contacted, and I was told to wait because the contractions were too far apart. I was again experiencing this type of pain, penetrating through my heart, while I waited for my daughter to arrive home.

Earlier that Saturday afternoon, campus detectives made a public statement that they did not have anything to go on and they were looking into the possibility of foul play but had no clues. They made mention that the Mississippi Bureau of Investigation was also assisting with the investigation. This was the first time something of this magnitude had happened in our small town. All the people were concerned over the loss of a missing child. What an image to see the communities working together as a part of God's plan for us: "to do unto others as you would have them do unto you." Luke 6:31 Nonetheless, the statements that were given at this point had no real value. How ironic that the statement given by the gas station attendant suggested that I kidnapped my own child; he could not give a description of me or the car I was supposed to be driving because he did not know me. I must say, though, that living in this small town, I chose to be particular of the people I associated with, so there weren't many who were acquainted with me. Yet hateful individuals continued to hinder the investigation by making reports to officials to stop looking for the missing child because she had been found. I did not make any of the calls because this was not true.

Sunday, May 10, the investigation continued of other family members. The authorities knocked on the door of my sister's home in rural Mississippi. My sister and I have different personalities, just as any siblings do. She is more outspoken with her opinions when it comes to her personal space. She looked out the front window to see who it was. In the light rain, she saw three plainclothesmen. She asked who it was.

One of them replied, "City police detectives."

Prior to opening the door, she cut the central air-conditioning off. She didn't feel the need to make them comfortable when she let them in. She preferred they say what they had to say and leave. She opened the door, asked if she could help them, and let them in.

One of the detectives gave his name and asked, "Can we ask you a few questions? Are you Kenya Smith's aunt?"

She replied she was.

He continued with his questioning: "When did you last see Kenya?" As she was preparing to answer the question, he immediately asked another: "Is she here in this house?"

Surprised at what had been said and annoyed, my sister said no. Remembering our conversation, she asked, "Do you want to take a look around?"

The same detective answered no, next asking, "Can we take a picture of you?"

Now really irritated my sister said yes, wondering why they wanted a photo. She did not have anything to hide. The photo was taken, and the men left the premises.

Tamika quickly made contact with me, furious to let me know what had happened, asking, "Why are they hassling us?"

The only thing I could say was that I believed they thought we had something to do with Kenya's disappearance.

One particular family member, Aunt Sug, my mother's sister, lived in the state of New Jersey, the place where I was born. Derek had the pleasure to meet her one year and sent her holiday greetings. He conveniently gave her address to the detectives leading the investigation. They passed the information on to the city's police department, who, skipping the pleasantries, banged on Aunt Sug's door early Monday morning and insisted they search the home.

"We're looking for a missing child named Kenya, and we have reason to believe she is here."

They searched from the attic to the basement. They got excited when they discovered Aunt Sug's daughter Kym in her bedroom. She wasn't feeling well on this particular day, and her parents allowed her to stay home from school. Sadly, Aunt Sug had to prove Kym was her daughter by showing them family photos. Once they saw they were at a dead end, they apologized for the search.

"Sorry, we were told to check out a lead."

Subsequently officers questioned relatives and searched the homes of family in the state of California, where Kenya was born, only to come up empty-handed again. In north Mississippi, at my Aunt Joyce's house, her daughter Jay was mistaken as Kenya, who was just six months older. The wild-goose chase was on as all the leads the detectives had failed.

After the unsuccessful visits to my relatives, later that evening I was called to report to the city police department to take a polygraph test. At this point I was exhausted and I just wanted to find my child. I didn't have anything to hide. Just maybe they could get on with the investigation and stop intruding on my family as the culprits. I was glad that I was reared in the way that I should go. A song had come to mind: "Victory, victory shall be mine. Victory, victory shall be mine. If I hold my peace and let the Lord fight my battle, victory shall be mine." The polygraph proved I did not know anything about Kenya's disappearance.

As time seemed stagnant, I started wondering why this was happening. *What have I done that God* has allowed this to happen? I understood that he was a merciful God and that there was a purpose for this to happen, but I could not understand the reason.

My first thought took me back to a few months prior, when I aborted a child. My younger child, Carlos, was three years old, and I was financially unable to care for another child. Selfishly I made the decision to get rid of the fetus as if the unborn child had no purpose. How my heart grieved after reading the literature describing how life starts at conception and the biblical Scriptures to support it. Many negative emotions started to culminate inside me, such as grief, guilt, anger, shame, and regret. I now was secretly blaming myself, in spite of the investigation.

As I continued to spiral into depression, I really did not know what to do. But I thank God that I knew of his existence, and I also thank him for the people he placed in my path during this time. For instance, Mrs. Thomas was a Sunday schoolteacher where I was first baptized as a member of Morning Light Baptist Church in New Jersey. She was now living in the neighboring state of Georgia. She had seen on the local news that a child was missing. She did not think much of it at first, though her heart went out to the family; but as the story unfolded, she was contacted by a daughter telling her that she knew who the mother was. Mrs. Thomas, unsure, obtained more details to find that she did know the family and planned a visit to our small town in Mississippi.

On the fifth day of Kenya's disappearance during a quiet moment as I sat waiting on the telephone to ring, there was a tapping on the door. I answered, and to my surprise, it was the Thomas family, Mr. and Mrs. Thomas and their daughter Glenda. What a pleasant turn of events. The first thing she said after the pleasantries was, "Now I know you remember what I taught you about the word of God. He will never put more on you than you can bear." At the time I did not know how powerful that spoken word was. She continued to encourage me and show me love and kindness.

God had people in place who would come and share his word with me so I would not fall into depression. Yet there were only two other individuals who came by to share encouragement through the biblical Word.

> be strong and of good courage do not be afraid, nor be dismayed, for the Lord your God is with you wherever you go. (Josh. 1:9)

Despite the encouragement from these people sent to me by Godbv, I still blamed myself because Kenya had gotten to where she did not want to go, to her father and stepmother's house. She preferred to visit his mother's house. She said that her stepmother, Bessie, was mean to her, doing things when her father was not around. For example, Bessie would pull her hair for no reason. And on occasion Bessie would pinch her. Kenya actually threw a tantrum before her prior visitation with her father because she did not want to go with her stepmother, who arrived to pick her up. Her paternal grandmother had been unable to come on that particular Friday to pick Kenya up for her weekend visit with her father. I stood there and allowed Bessie to make the threat that she would call Derek if Kenya did not come along with her. As a result, Kenya calmed down, but I should have just delayed letting her go because I felt my daughter wasn't welcome by the stepmother in their home.

For the last six months there had been a problem with the parental relationship. If I said to Derek that Kenya had made a statement about the stepmother, he suggested I was not being truthful, and the next week he would make statements about my husband, Kevin. I never thought that it would result in something like this. I just wanted my baby back, and that was all that mattered.

"Lord, please help me!" I was trying not to lose my mind as I sat patiently, not leaving my home, waiting for the phone to ring so I could hear Kenya's voice once again.

CHAPTER 3

Missing Child

May 12, Missing Child Case # 05870038—was the number given by the Bureau of investigation that a child was missing. This was what my daughter had been reduced to—a number, along with the other statistics of missing children. Each night seemed just as long as the days; I was unable to sleep, not knowing what had happened to Kenya. Would she be held for a ransom, who was she with, and what was going on? Questioning as I continued to wait for the telephone to ring. I was sure of one thing only, and that was that Kenya knew her telephone number. Tenaciously I waited as my thoughts raced through my head, one after another, wondering when this would be over. As the people of the community proceeded to show expressions of sympathy in the search for Kenya, I did not want to believe that Kenya was gone. I had not heard anything, and I was not going to give up hope that she would be found. I felt she was somewhere safe.

I tried to watch television to keep my mind occupied, though I found myself watching the phone more. There was always someone with me despite the fact that I was considered by the police as a suspect. I was also agitated because people started asking questions, not out of concern for Kenya but for information about what had happened. Other than what news reports had specified at the time, I knew nothing, and I was not concerned with hearsay because the people talking did not know me. For instance, while standing in line at the local grocery store, I witnessed two young ladies prattling, "Girl, I heard ..." calling me everything but a child of God. They did not realize that the very person they were speaking of was standing at the next register. I just kept my mouth shut and went on my way because I did not want to waste time away from home. I felt exhausted and helpless, not knowing any details.

The search had expanded, and the stepmother's statement was given to the media in response to Kenya's disappearance. "Kenya was taking a bath at the apartment about 1:00 p.m.," Chief Green announced. "We've covered the entire wooded area on foot and with tracking dogs near the campus apartments, covering a range of 4.6 miles. After questioning the stepmother, detectives have reason to believe foul play was involved." Fliers were distributed throughout the community as the search continued. There were no signs of Kenya—only flagrant rumors.

> Preserve me, O God: for in thee do I put my trust. (Ps. 16:1)

CHAPTER 4

A New Perspective

On May 14 at 10:45 a.m., I received a call from the city detective Charles Martin. He wanted to know if he could come out and talk with me about Kenya. I quickly asked if she was found. He stated no, he just wanted to talk to me; so the appointment was made for 12:00 noon the next day. Someone finally wanted to know how I was feeling!

The top of the hour approached, and right on time there was a knock at the door. I opened it to see a tall, slender-built man with blue jeans and cowboy boots, who politely said, "Are you Nicole Dean?"

"Yes," I responded.

"I am Officer Martin."

I invited him in. I was elated to have him visit with me to get to know the child I knew.

The interview covered Kenya's personality. I described her as intelligent and even clever at times; she was all I would expect her to be as a child learning to become her own person. A loving child, but one who was very particular about people who were strangers. I went on to say that I thought it was strange that she would just take off because she would cry and go into a panic if we were distant in the grocery store while she was procrastinating in the cereal or snack food aisles. She did not ever want to be left alone anywhere. The officer was pleased to hear this and went on to say that he was aware of the subpoena I had gotten on the ninth, the day of Kenya's disappearance. I told him that the officer who gave it to me said that it was for an increase in child support, but the detective said that it may have been a petition for custody of Kenya and that her father, Derek, was trying to pursue a child abuse case. I was shocked. How could he?

The detective went on discussing the particulars, first asking about Kenya's relationship with her stepmother. A lightbulb came on, and I thought about the things Kenya had told me about the visits and how her stepmother was treating her when her father was not around, not to mention the tantrum she had prior to the last visit when her stepmother came to pick her up. Next, he asked how Derek felt when I would confront him about things she may have done.

"He did not want to hear it. He always had a remark about my husband. On one particular visit, Kenya returned home with burns on her buttocks.

Commencement

Derek stated she had taken a bath and backed into the heater. Oh really, she understood the difference in hot and cold. I didn't call the Department of Human Resources, but maybe I should have."

Out of concern for my daughter, I had secretly conducted my own investigation such as would have been made by the Department of Human Resources. I shared the information with my dear friend Wynette, who was a child services social worker. Arrangements were made for Kenya to have lunch with her son R. J. While dining at Fun Burger, she would talk with Kenya to discover if the allegations of Kevin abusing Kenya were in fact inaccurate. I was pleased to find out that they were not true.

This concluded the interview, and Detective Martin assured me from this point he would be working in close proximity with me, discussing details of the case and responding to the public as the search continued. His last words were that the city detectives were working in full cooperation with campus detectives for the duration of the investigation.

> In my distress I cried unto the Lord and
> he heard me. (Ps. 120:1)

To my surprise a $10,000.00 reward was offered May 15 by the mayor's office. I was very hopeful that this might bring about a good lead to the whereabouts of Kenya. I was filled with gratitude that the money was put up by the mayor's office because I could have never put up that kind of money. If anyone had any information, they were to contact Captain Pete Hilliard because every lead would be followed up.

Nonetheless, a statement from Chief Green was issued on May 17: "Leads were checked as far away as New Jersey and California, but so far have turned up nothing. I never have seen a case where there was not even a single piece of evidence, not even a fiber or hair sample." A number of things could have been done in the three hours prior to reporting Kenya missing. For example, the crime area could have been cleaned of any evidence. My heart was heavy; I felt as if I were in a perpetual state of numbness. I couldn't eat and couldn't sleep, waiting for answers as time slowly drifted by.

> For whatever things were written before were written for our learning, that we through the patience and comfort of the Scriptures might have hope. (Rom.15:4)

PART TWO

Shattered

CHAPTER 5

Facing Reality

The stench of flesh brought forth the truth. On May 19 at 8:45 p.m., Detective Martin was at the door once again. He said he had some news about Kenya and asked if he could come in.

Anxiously I asked, "What is it?" He wasn't excited, and there was not a smile on his face.

Detective Martin asked me to have a seat. He calmly said Kenya had been found. I quickly stood up wanting to scream; I was stunned that she was found dead. Although I was relieved to have an answer, my heart dropped to the bottom of my stomach. I froze in time as he continued to talk. I tried to listen as the tears streamed down my face. Suddenly I began to make derogatory remarks concerning any person who could do such a thing; my husband and the detective tried to console me. I finally calmed down, not wanting to speak of it again. The detective wanted me to know the whole story before it was made public by the media. So I sat down once again to listen, but I wasn't really paying attention. I was in a daze.

Kenya was found by a jogger named Adam Knox at 5:30 p.m. on a dirt road off Fretter's Mill Road, which runs east of Plantation Road in a rural section of our town. Kenya was in a green trash bag, naked, with only her barrettes in her hair, with body parts detached from her decomposing body. Detective Martin asked if I remembered how her hair was combed and the type of barrettes she had in her hair. I slowly answered yes and described that she had three ponytails, one in the top and two on the bottom; then I told him her hair was like it was in the fliers, with oval-shaped barrettes on the ends of each ponytail. Next he asked for any extra bows that matched the ones in her hair to be used for a positive identification because he did not feel it would be good for me to see her in the decomposed state, but he assured me it was a little girl fitting Kenya's description.

On May 20 the headlines read "Missing Girl Has Been Found." Chief Green of the university police and Captain Hilliard of the city police made statements that they did have a suspect in the case but declined to release any names. Green did speak of family members being involved, so there was no need for public alarm. Hilliard indicated that there was no child snatcher involved in this case, and

Commencement

Chief Luther told the press no one had been charged as of press time, but foul play was indicated. The investigation was to continue by the Mississippi Department of Forensic Sciences, where the body was sent for an autopsy.

On Saturday, May 23, a memorial was given at Trinity Baptist Church, my family's church; since the burial arrangements were made by Derek, I was given a message that the services could be held at our church. This was not a traditional funeral service, where people come into the sanctuary and view the body in a casket to bid their farewells before being seated. Instead, there was an eleven-by-sixteen photo placed on the communion table covered with a beige tablecloth because the body was still under the care of the state forensics department. The children's choir Kenya had enjoyed singing with rendered a selection. I was somewhat glad that there was not a body. It allowed me to hold onto the thought that she was still near. Quietly I cried while leaning into my husband's shoulder, not wanting to look up or to have to face the fact that I was at a funeral for my child, pretending that it was not real since the body was not there. Community support was overwhelming; there was standing room only, and the overflow had to wait in the fellowship hall. However, I was waiting for the body to be released before I could say good-bye.

On May 26 the body was finally released. A graveside service was planned for the next day, on May 27, my birthday. The media was asked not to inform the public until after the services. I wanted fewer spectators during the final hour. However, this day really got to me because I did not want to face it. I procrastinated because no one was around to say hurry up. My mother had called me about eight o'clock to make sure I was up. Time seemed as if it was going by faster than usual, and the service was planned for 11:00 a.m., but I just couldn't seem to shake my mood. I was like a time bomb waiting to explode. When I couldn't find my wedding ring the ignition went off. I let out a loud scream, I kicked, I stomped, and I grabbed a pillow and screamed some more because the phone was not going to ring—my baby was gone.

My husband and I were supposed to meet at my parents' house at ten thirty, but we hadn't yet arrived. It goes without saying that they left without us to go to the grave site. Thank God, it was just five minutes from their house. I finally got myself together, and when my husband and I arrived, it was 11:20 a.m. There people there waiting patiently; there were others who looked as if they wanted to say, "What took you so long?"

The service began with a song, and her body was committed to the earth, followed by a prayer,

Commencement

and it was over. This day will never have the same pleasurable, happy birthday to me. I bade a brokenhearted farewell to my firstborn as I watched them lower her body into the grave. I tossed in a flower just as the dirt was being placed over the casket, standing there in silence as I stared at the place that would be her new resting place.

When we returned to my parents' house, I thanked those who had come for the service. My family members all laughed as my mother said, "I can't believe you were late. You will probably be late for your own funeral." Then someone calmly said, "Everything will be all right; things heal in time."

> I will lift up mine eyes unto the hills,
> from whence cometh my help. (Ps. 121:1)

CHAPTER 6

Starting Over

The worst had happened. My vision had come to pass, and I was in distress living in a small town in Mississippi. A week later after all was said and done, my cousin Deanne came to visit me, and a welcome visit that was. She had been one of the first to see Kenya when she was born and was like a big sister to me. Upon her arrival she was instrumental in finalizing funeral arrangements, in particular in choosing Kenya's headstone and how I wanted it to read. I wanted something heartfelt, something with a purpose. I finally decided on "Victorious in the End." There were unwarranted comments made simply because I was misunderstood. It was said I had made reference to the charges against the perpetrator. And that was the furthest thing from my mind.

During Deanne's visit while we were talking, she asked, "Where is your Bible?" I was embarrassed to say I didn't have one. She was stunned because she felt I knew better and should have had one, so before the visit was over, I was given my first Bible in November 1987, a needed necessity. Though it gave me a sense of comfort to have a Bible, I was very uncomfortable living in a place I once thought would be safe for my family; I did not know that devastation's path would find me in a small town in Mississippi.

Unsure of my surroundings, my family and I moved from that small Mississippi town to the neighboring state of Georgia, hoping this would alleviate the numbness and emptiness I felt in my heart. My husband and I, along with our three-year-old, moved into an apartment complex in Atlanta, and we both maintained jobs. We were not alone. A close friend of my husband and other siblings also lived there. They had suggested we move there for employment opportunities. Regrettably, we were only there for a short time.

The change in scenery did me good, but it did not still my aching heart. Eventually I had a dream of Kenya in a white dress she wore one year for Easter, waiting as I came out of a brick building. There she stood, and I called out to her. It was so real. She softly said, "I am okay, Mama. Don't worry about me. I'll see you again." I ran to give her a hug but once I let go, she was gone. I awakened with a wet pillowcase and eyes full of tears.

In that moment on May 19, one year after the day Kenya was found, something changed in me. I received a release. God had finally lifted the burden from my heart. I was able to accept the fact that my daughter was not coming back. There was no mistaking that she was in the casket, never to be seen again. Once I came to my senses, I realized she had given me another message. She would see me again. My thought went back to the word of God, which tells us that children go to heaven.

In that instant I had an epiphany. I knew what I must do if I wanted to see her again. I admitted that my going to church may have been just a routine. I had no real relationship with God, and that had to change if I wanted to make it to where my daughter was. A week after that visitation, I found that I was pregnant. After the fifth month, I developed some complications. Unable to continue to work, I was placed on bed rest. Having feelings of unease, I wanted to be close to my mother, so we moved back to Mississippi. This time we went to the county seat of Monroe County.

> Then Jesus called a little child to Him, set him in the midst of them, and said, "Assuredly, I say to you, unless you are converted and become as little children, you will by no means enter the kingdom of heaven. (Matt. 18:2–3)

PART THREE

Mending the Pieces

CHAPTER 7

Seeking Change

I was not living a life consistent with how I was raised; I was living by my thoughts and emotions. I was spiritually drifting. I had a responsibility to study the Word of God so that I might have a better understanding of life's adversity. For it is written in Romans, chapter 8, verse 28, that "all things work together for good to them that love God, to them who are the called according to his purpose." What was my purpose?

Ignorant of God's will for my life, I thought of material things and earthly titles, but as I continued to seek the word written in the Holy Bible, I discovered in 2 Timothy, chapter 2, verse 15, that I should study "to show myself approved unto God, a workman that needeth not to be ashamed, rightly dividing the word of truth." And from this I would learn of my purpose. An individual at some point in life wonders, *Why, why am I here?* To answer that question, I needed a good foundation. I chose to use my Bible to resolve the question.

The more I learned of it, the better I understood. For instance, as the creator of heaven and earth, he is an all-knowing God, who stated in Jeremiah, chapter 1, verse 5: "Before I formed you in the womb I knew you; and before you came forth out of the womb I sanctified you, and I ordained you." Here I perceived that we all have a purpose that has been ordained by God. How awesome to know that before you are born you had a pure heart uncorrupted, uninfluenced by the ways of the world. We all are born as a blessing to our parents from God, regardless of how we are conceived. God allows things to happen for a reason unknown to mankind.

In my search for answers, I did not always comprehend what was being said. Yet Luke, chapter 8, verse 10, presented me with, "To you it has been given to know the mysteries of the kingdom of God, but to the rest it is given in parables." A parable is a short story that illustrates a moral attitude or a religious principle. I had to study, or the parables' meanings would be limited to my understanding.

I further found that in chapter 3, of Ephesians, the answer to the mystery is the Holy Spirit; that was how I was going to know God's purpose for me. I had to be filled with the Holy Spirit, just as Paul was, in order to have the purpose of God revealed to me. So, how was I going to be filled with the Holy Spirit? Acts, chapter 2, verse 38, states: "Then Peter said unto them, Repent [regret any past actions of wrongdoing], and be baptized every one of you in the name of Jesus Christ for the remission of sins, and ye shall receive the gift of the Holy Ghost." You must reveal all your wrongdoings to God to be forgiven, no matter how long ago it has been, to receive his gift. Being baptized is being submerged in water, which represents a watery grave from which you will rise again a new person, a believer, just as Jesus did when he came up out from his grave. Oh, what a mighty God we serve. He gives us an opportunity to discover our purpose through Jesus Christ; not only does he give us the opportunity, but he gives us directions from individuals who are not perfect but who have learned to walk with Christ, to live according to the word of God.

Paul was adamant in 1 Corinthians, chapter 15, that to become more like Christ, your flesh must die daily, meaning your old way of thinking must die. He further states in Romans, chapter 12, verse 2, "Be not conformed to this world: but be ye transformed by the renewing of your mind, that ye may prove what is that good, and acceptable, and perfect will of God." As a result, my heart and mind would be changed to please God; this would be a daily quest. My journey would commence with a transformation.

> Train up a child in the way he should go: and when he is old, he will not depart from it. (Prov. 22:6)

CHAPTER 8

New Life

In January 1990, back in our small town in Mississippi visiting at my parents' home, my water broke at 6:30 a.m., and my contractions started coming quickly. I took a shower because I did not want to smell. I made it to the hospital. I had dilated eight centimeters. I barely made it to the delivery room, the pains coming so rapidly I did not know my own strength. As I pushed, I broke one of the bedside rails. The staff was shocked, but at 8:35 a.m., a healthy nine-pound, thirteen-ounce baby boy was born.

I wondered what I should name him because I was hoping for a girl. I had plenty of names for girls, but not a one for him. My son was known as baby Dean because I could not think of a name to fit him. He did not get a name until the day of discharge. I wanted to be careful choosing his name. I wanted it to have meaning, so I searched the Bible to find a name and chose David, meaning beloved. My heavenly Father was truly with me because I had a safe delivery. You see, I was told by the doctor that if I had not gone on bed rest, there was a chance that I would not make it through the birth of my baby or the child would not make it through the delivery. Hallelujah, death was defeated.

Months later, I found myself dragging my feet as a follower of Christ. I had become a backslider; my spiritual life was gone, and I was only calling on God when I needed something from him. I eventually learned that the situations that occurred in my life were all because I wasn't devoted in my pursuit of Christ. Even though he had given me grace and mercy, my burdens were heavy. Proverbs, chapter 28, verse 13, explains: "He that covereth his sins shall not prosper: but whoso confesseth and forsaketh them shall have mercy." I knew of God's word, and I did nothing. The Scripture further states, "Come to me, all you who are weary and burdened, and I will give you rest. Take my yoke upon you and learn from me, for I am gentle and humble in heart, and you will find rest for your souls. For my yoke is easy and my burden is light" (Matt. 11:28–30).

I had to get back to the path that God had for me. The Scripture explains. "wide is the gate and broad *is* the way that leads to destruction, and there are many who go in by it, because narrow *is* the gate and difficult *is* the way which leads to life, and there are few who find it" (Matt. 7:13–14). I had good intentions, but that was not enough. I had to realize that God's word never changes. This is evident in Hebrews, chapter 13, verse 8: "Jesus Christ *is* the same yesterday, today, and forever."

For that reason, I should not be fearful with my commitment as a follower of Christ. I must learn to walk by faith and not by what I see, developing a personal relationship with Christ. Though he gives us grace, which is an infinite love and a capacity to tolerate our faults, he also gives us mercy, which always forgives others. On the other hand, he allows things to happen in our lives to get our attention. He allows things to happen in our lives to see what choices we will make. Will we seek his ways or ours?

> For my thoughts are not your thoughts,
> neither are your ways my ways, saith
> the Lord. (Isa. 55:8)

PART FOUR

Closure

CHAPTER 9

Recommencement

These were times of emotional despair for me, taking one day at a time, secretly still mourning the death of my child on every Mother's Day and every birthday. Still in my small town in Mississippi after the birth of my son, I had not gotten back to the capital city. Conversation of Kenya was null and void at this time. I had no discussion for anyone once I laid her body to rest; the only time I spoke of Kenya again was during the trial.

At the Webb County Justice Center, spectators filled the room, but the double doors were closed for me; I was not allowed in the courtroom until it was my turn to testify. Not only was I waiting, but those who were to make a statement remained outside as well; I stood in silence with butterflies in my stomach anticipating the call from the bailiff. However, on the third day, the court trial was called a mistrial because one of the jurors stated she was no longer comfortable listening to the evidence of the case, which revealed Kenya was found dead and wrapped in garbage bags. According to the newspaper, Judge Alfred D. Price said he had no choice but to declare a mistrial after being informed a member of the jury had become "emotionally or mentally" unable to continue through the trial and render a fair verdict. Subsequently, she was found out to have been a relative of the accused.

Disappointed the trial was going to be prolonged, feelings of unease arose in me. I had to find the strength to move on by keeping myself occupied and taking one day at a time. Still having feelings of anger toward Derek and Bessie, I just wanted to remain as far away from them as possible. During this time silence was golden. The next court date was set for the next session, which was in the following year, in February 1988, so until that time I had to wait patiently for justice to prevail.

Court resumed on February 19 without a glitch. Again I waited in the lobby in front of courtroom 3 until my testimony was needed. Finally, the truth would be revealed. I was told by the DA's assistant Katie Lovejoy that the trial might last all week due to the witnesses and evidence that needed to be presented. However, the most profound statement would be from the jogger who discovered the body. I was unaware of the graphic details involved, and I was told that it would be in my best interest not to see the photos of where she was found; on the other hand, I was only given the opportunity to identify Kenya by the way her hair was combed and the barrettes in her hair. Katie, as I was told to call the assistant, was a big help while going through this ordeal; she was there for me as if she were my best friend, and yet I had never met her before this incident. I needed that, being the last witness to speak.

Finally, the trial was on its last day. The jury had to make the decision of Bessie Smith's fate under the laws of the earth, but I knew that there was a higher being that would give the final judgment. My hope was based on faith that if she were guilty, she would not go unpunished. The deliberation took some time as the jurors meticulously reviewed the evidence presented. In her statement, Bessie reportedly told how she pretended to show Kenya how to swim in the bathtub. According to that statement, Bessie held Kenya's head under water too long and then panicked.

The time had come. My heartbeat was racing as the foreman said, "We find the defendant not guilty of murder." My heart dropped to my stomach. I was thinking, *How can this be?* But the final decision was yet to come. The foreman then said, "For the charge of manslaughter, we find the defendant guilty." I was in awe, yet relieved. It was further clarified how they arrived at that conclusion. Because it was done in the heat of the moment rather than premeditated, Bessie was found guilty of manslaughter and sentenced to ten years in prison.

On October 13, 1993, at 9:00 a.m., I received a telephone call from my mother stating that Derek Smith would like to talk with me. I asked if she knew why. She said no. Since my mother had two-way calling, I asked her to call him back to witness the conversation. The phone rang, and I asked to speak with him. We skipped the pleasantries, and he asked if I was told Bessie was out of prison.

"No!" I responded. Frustrated, I got off the phone and immediately made contact with the district attorney's office to ask why I wasn't informed that Bessie was released. I spoke with Mrs. Carmichael from the District Attorney's office, and she was just as surprised because their office wasn't informed either. I then asked who I needed to speak with, and she directed me to Monroe, Mississippi, to the Board of Corrections Office to get an explanation of why Bessie was released.

The next morning I met with a young lady who gave me this explanation: Bessie got out on a good-time release because her sentencing was not a class-A felony. She was only sentenced to ten years, and her time served after her arrest was counted toward her sentencing; after five years if a person has had good behavior, the individual is eligible for parole. Disappointed with what I heard, I felt cheated that my child's life was only worth five years, yet I took solace in knowing that Bessie still had to be judged by God. It is written "if our heart condemns us, God is greater than our heart, and knoweth all things" (1 John 3:20).

Carlos was now my elder child, and David was my younger. I never thought life would be such toil. I planned to finish college before I started a family, to be financially stable and to provide for my family as my parents did for me. Kevin was working and so was I, but the struggle became overwhelming, for the ways of the world were influencing our spending habits and the dynamics of the family were changing, making it difficult to maintain an emotional relationship.

The year 1995 was the year of recommencing: I was ready to move on, to make a change in my life, starting with teaching my children in the way they should go. This started with a different church, which was smaller, so the children and I could grow with the church, developing a good rapport with its members. However, a deacon from our family's church where the funeral services were held had become a minister while I was absent from the church. He was asked to minister at a newly established church. My sister and I went to hear him speak, and I decided I would return along with my family. It was easy to support this church because the pastor was also from our neighborhood and he was known as an upstanding citizen.

As the word of God went forth, I participated with the Sunday school department, youth choir, and ushering. I had gotten back into the practice of things. I was reaffirmed on how to be a good steward, and also I had learned the importance of paying my tithes and offerings. It felt good to be back in the house of the Lord working with its members, all in one accord, to get the work done. In August 1996, we completed the construction of our new church building. What a feeling to be a patron for the ministry. As my commitment grew, I realized I still had a cross to bear, having other duties to fulfill at home, being wife, mother, and employee, while upholding my position and representing the Telemetry department on the policy and procedure committee. Still, the empty void in my heart had not been filled. What did I have to do to be freed of this emptiness?

In March 1998 my mother-in-law became ill, and my husband was making weekly visits to her. One day we decided to move back to Monroe, where we initially planned to be. Kevin started his job search, employment came through quickly, and we were on

Commencement

our way back to the capital city. Because the job he had gotten wanted him to start immediately, we moved in for a short time with his mother. However, work for me was slow, so I remained on my job, commuting on the weekends not only to work but to church as well. I did not want to leave my church family. But I knew one day it would have to end. I wanted to remain faithful with my commitment to God.

Once we moved from my mother-in-law's home, I continued to visit her, making sure she was doing okay. On one particular visit, she stated she had a doctor's appointment that week and no one seemed to be able to take her. I said that I would take her because I was working weekends only. We arrived at her appointment on time, and while waiting for her to finish with her visit, I was talking with the receptionist about employment in their office. He said they were not hiring at this time but it never hurt to put in an application. So I did. The next day I got a phone call to come in for an interview, and the rest was history.

God had blessed me with a job at the cardiovascular clinic. I knew it was him moving on my behalf because the workers were surprised when I showed up, telling me they didn't know the company was hiring for the position I had gotten. Hallelujah! God blessed me with job stability for the next fourteen years. This was evidence for me: "seek first the kingdom of heaven and all things shall be added unto you" (Matt. 6:33). In spite of my period of unemployment, I did not let it discourage me to make me renege on God.

I finally turned in my resignation, ending the commute, but the most difficult thing I had to do was find a church home in the town in which I lived. Being of Baptist affiliation, I would visit churches, but I was not moved to join any of them. In the meantime, I was watching a televangelist on the East Coast who caught my attention with his message of the mystery of God's word and the Holy Ghost, something I had never heard before, though it was referenced in the Bible. I did not remember hearing from a previous pastor to read it for myself. This way you can learn without being influenced by an individual's opinion.

So every Sunday morning I looked forward to the televangelist, but I felt uncomfortable watching him on television and sending my tithes to my hometown church. God was dealing with me to get off the couch and find a church to go to. My problem was finding the love and kindness of my previous church; if I didn't feel the love, I didn't go back. Alas, this was something I had to do, for the Scripture says not to "forsake the assembling of ourselves together, that we may encourage one another" (Heb. 10:25). I just had to find a local church to attend.

Commencement

I was in a funk. Carlos was a senior in high school, and David was in junior high school.

I wanted to find something to occupy my time. So, I started night classes at a local university, and seeking the Lord was limited to televangelists. During this time Kevin had become functionally independent from the family. We were slowly spiraling downward. The words found in Mark, chapter 4, verse 19, made it clear to me that the cares of this world, the deceitfulness of riches, and the desires for other things entering in choke the Word, and it becomes unfruitful.

I assume that God finally said, "Enough is enough." I got a fretful call one evening from a young lady whom Carlos had gone out with for a group outing. She explained that her male cousin, who was Carlos's friend, was upset because his date had to meet a curfew, being close to his house he got out of the car wanting to walk home because he did not want his date to leave. Carlos got out behind him, pleading with him to get back in the car. Before that could happen, they were hit by oncoming traffic. My heart dropped to the bottom of my stomach when she said he wasn't breathing and had been transported to the local hospital.

All the feeling of the loss of my first child came back, and all I knew to do was pray, asking the Lord, "Please, don't take him too." God had my attention.

Once I got to the hospital and found he was alive in CCU, nothing else mattered. Due to the extent of his injuries, he was stabilized and transferred to Children's Hospital. Once again death was defeated. I knew God would bring him through because all things were working for my good.

> For I know the thoughts that I think toward you, says the LORD, thoughts of peace and not of evil, to give you a future and a hope. (Jer. 29:11)

CHAPTER 10

Transforming

One day Kevin saw an old childhood friend. After catching up on their lives, he discovered his old friend had become a pastor of a church, and he now invited Kevin to an outdoor revival. I was glad to hear that Kevin had spoken with a man of God. Excited about seeing his friend, he wanted me to also come to the revival, but I wasn't feeling up to par so I told him to go without me. I knew that God was up to something. I was sincerely hoping that this would make a change in his lifestyle. Kevin was the type if he said he was going to do something for a friend, he would make sure that he did it. After the service Kevin came home with a family invitation for Sunday service. I wanted to know more about the service he attended. All he said was, "He's a good preacher; you'll like him." They were a nondenominational church that practiced Holiness.

Carlos was recovering from the accident. His pelvis was in traction for eight weeks. It was time for me to do what I knew best, serve the Lord. Who knows? Maybe this was God's answer to my prayers for a church home. I had never been to a nondenominational church before, so I wasn't sure what to expect. I was only aware of the ignorance that was said about Holiness people: that they were loud, they practiced talking in tongues, and if no one could understand them, they were not truly speaking, and the oil they put on you was mixed with something to make you pass out. Yet I remembered what the televangelist had said about the Holy Ghost, and I needed the Holy Ghost to get to heaven.

Kevin asked again if I wanted to go to his friend's church. I said no. He asked twice, and both times I said no. The third time he asked, I felt compelled to go because I didn't want to be the reason he wouldn't go. So, Sunday morning, the entire family went to Faith Works Church of God, a storefront church, which was fine with me because I knew how it was starting a new church. The pastor preached a great sermon, but what really got my attention was the summation after the service about what it takes to give your life to Christ. It was unlike anything I ever heard. It really made me think about the commitments I had previously made and why I was able to backslide so easily.

So I went back again. Sunday became every Sunday, as well as Tuesday night's Bible study. I

Commencement

would call my sister in Christ Wynette, who was already of the faith, and share with her the things that I was learning and how I was thinking about joining. She told me how she was praying for her friends and family to come into the faith. Look at how God works. He will put people in your life to make sure you will eventually get where he wants you to be. Faith Works became God's ram in the bush for me to get back to his word.

> Open my eyes, that I may behold wondrous things out of your law. (Ps. 119:18)

In 2003 I became a member of Faith Works. I stood at the altar naked in humility as Eve stood in the garden, exposed. I was rebaptized because I wanted to be in the will of God according to Paul's writings in Acts, chapter 19, which asks a question: "Did you receive the Holy Ghost when you believed?" For me the answer was no. It further states that Paul asks, "into what were you baptized." Paul explains that "John indeed baptized with a baptism of repentance," saying to the people that they should believe in Christ Jesus. When they heard this, they were baptized (again) in the name of the Lord Jesus. And when Paul had laid hands on them, the Holy Spirit came upon them, and they spoke with tongues. Peter also confirms that I should repent and be baptized—"every one of you in the name of Jesus Christ for the remission of sins, and ye shall receive the gift of the Holy Ghost." (Acts 19: 2-5)

I was disappointed after baptism. I had the Holy Ghost without the evidence of speaking in tongues, yet this was all new to me and I wasn't discouraged. The following Sunday I had an utterance. I wasn't quite there. The next Sunday, which was the second week after the baptism, David and I went to church. On this particular Sunday, everyone got up to shake the pastor's hand after the sermon. As I went by, he called me back and said, "It's on you. If you believe, you will receive it." There I was, the only one at the altar calling on the name of Jesus, and lo and behold, the pastor put a microphone to my mouth for the audience to hear. I was saved with the evidence of speaking in tongues. What a joyful day!

The Scripture confirms "that as many as received him, to them gave he power to become the sons of God, even to them that believe on his name" (John 1:12). I had never experienced anything like it, and I didn't have to practice it and the oil didn't make me pass out. The Scripture further tells me in Romans, chapter 8, verse 9, that I am not in the flesh, "but in the Spirit, if so be that the Spirit of God dwells in me. Now if any man have not the Spirit of Christ, he is none of his." I had now been redeemed by the blood of Jesus Christ.

I was now sanctified. Nevertheless, this didn't mean every day was going to be trouble-free. Pivotal times are part of one's spiritual journey. The enemy will use people in the church as well as the streets, but the good thing about God is he will never leave or forsake us. I have the Comforter, which is the Holy Ghost. He shall teach me all things and bring all things to my remembrance, "whatsoever I have said unto you," (John 14:26) meaning the word of God, what is righteous, what is true. So when adversities come my way, I pray, step back, and let God have his way. Once again I was working with the ushers, choir, and youth choir. Things were going well. I was learning what God expected of me. It is written Jesus was sent "to open their eyes, and to turn them from darkness to light, and from the power of Satan unto God, that they may receive forgiveness of sins, and inheritance among them which are sanctified by faith that is in me" (Acts 26:18).

On May 19, 2007, I realized that twenty years had passed since the death of Kenya, in particular, the day her body was found. I got a phone call from a niece who was in town at the shopping mall with a friend, and she asked if it was okay for her to bring her friend to my home. I didn't think much of it, so I said that it would be fine. I thought it was a male friend, so I asked her who her friend was because the boys were home and might have known him, but she said it was Kenya's sister Gina. I was surprised to hear the name of Kenya's half-sister, but it was too late to change my mind. *This is going to be awkward*, I thought. Unexpectedly God was working on me.

They shortly arrived at my home. As Gina walked through the door, I could see the resemblance to her mother. A rush of emotions came over me, but the grace of God kept me. All I could do at that moment was freeze where I stood as she slowly approached me for an introduction. The first thing that came to mind was that she was a baby and she had nothing to do with what had happened. So when she reached for me to get a hug, I responded back. She then started asking me questions about Kenya. She asked if she could see photos that I had. I didn't mind accommodating her because she was an injured party too. The visit was brief, yet long enough to answer questions she needed answered. This day had new meaning for Gina. She found a peace of mind from me. Look at God work.

On June 17 another move in the spirit took place. After the pastor's sermon, my grandson Dauris and I needed to pick up something from the hardware department, so we went to one of the local Walmarts.

As we browsed through the store, I glimpsed a young lady who looked like Gina, so I stopped and

Commencement

stepped back to look down the aisle I had just passed and I saw someone else. She had gray highlights in her hair, and as I got closer and closer, I recognized the face. I gasped for breath. The woman was not paying attention to me, so it seemed. I asked her if her name was Bessie, and she said yes. I then asked how she was. She responded she was fine. I asked if she knew who I was. I reached for her to give her a hug and whispered in her ear that I was Kenya's mother. "I forgive you," I said.

She immediately started to cry as we embraced each other.

I continued, "That is the past, and God knows what happened."

We stepped back and wiped the tears from our eyes. "You don't know how much this means to me," she said.

"Yes, I do."

"No, you really don't know how much this means to me," she said, still teary-eyed.

"It's all right," I said. "I am okay because I am a Christian and want to do the will of God."

Bessie asked what church I attended, and instead of giving her the name of my church, I just said, "Holiness."

"I can tell," she said.

Hallelujah! God had given me a release so that I could continue to grow through him. What a mighty

God we serve. It is written, "Judge not, and ye shall not be judged: condemn not, and ye shall not be condemned: forgive, and ye shall be forgiven" (Luke 6:37).

On December 31 I was looking forward to watching the night service, reflecting on how God was mending me through his spirit, and I realized I had one more part of this experience to complete. At work on break, I called information to get the telephone number of Mr. Derek Smith. I was ready to ask questions that I felt needed to be answered, but when the time came, the Lord said differently. Pleasantries were short; I said that I was at work so I needed to get to the point.

"I forgive you," abruptly came out of my mouth, "for how you treated me after we broke up and for the events that led to Kenya's death." I also pointed out, "You believed everything others had to say about me."

He replied, "Now I understand why you've never said anything to me."

The conversation ended in a dignified manner, and I have not spoken to him again. Forgiveness for me was the decision to do what was right before God. You see, if I had listened to humans, I might have done something foolish, for it is written: "Man lays a snare, but whoever trusts in the Lord is kept safe" (Prov. 29:25). We have learned in society to hold in our anger and been taught revenge, but we must make a decision to forgive in order to begin the healing process. Others can hinder your healing when they bring things to your thought process and interject their opinions.

Forgiveness is the most important part of the word of God, yet it's the most neglected. His word solidifies the connection between agape love and humans' definition of love. The love he has for me I must show toward others by forgiving. On the other hand, an individual can give the impression of the most loving and giving person, but secretly hold a grudge against someone until the day he or she dies. That's not right in the eyes of God. We are taught to forgive others as Jesus forgave us.

Do you realize that the sin of not forgiving will keep you from entering into heaven? For it is written in Matthew 7: 21 "Not everyone that saith unto me, Lord, Lord, shall enter into the kingdom of heaven; but he that doeth the will of my Father which is in heaven." Indeed, I wanted to see my daughter again, but most of all, I wanted to make it to heaven. I thank God for opening my eyes and showing me the way.

> Teach me your way, O Lord; I will walk in your truth; Unite my heart to fear your name. (Ps. 86:11)

CHAPTER 11

Testimony

While working for the cardiovascular group, I met many people. Many times a conversation would start by me asking, "How are you today?" I would try to keep them encouraged regardless of how they were feeling, and when the conversation shifted, I didn't mind saying, "In spite of my situation, God's been good to me."

Well, those words were said to a client who came in dressed casually. He had on a pair of blue jeans and a black Harley- Davidson T-shirt with black boots. He also had his daughter with him on his first visit with me. We exchanged pleasantries, and when asked how I was, I said my favorite words: "In spite of my situation, God is good to me," and I kept going on and on. He never once interrupted me. He just let me talk about the goodness of the Lord. Once I realized I had spoken too much, I asked if he would forgive me.

"I know that I am in the workplace, and you may not have the same beliefs."

He just smiled and said, "I don't mind; I was getting happy hearing you talk like that. I love to hear people talk about the Lord." He said to his daughter, who was sitting in the chair on the opposite side of me, "Ain't that right, Leah?" She smiled, agreeing with him. I finished the lab work he needed, and he was gone.

But the goodness of God revealed itself when a couple of days later, he came back looking for me. He spoke with my supervisor, RN Noble, a member of Sisters in Christ. He told her how he enjoyed our conversation and how the Lord put it on his heart to leave a message for me. Sister Noble was eager to contact me to inform me of the letter that was left for me, which she agreed to bring to me when she got off from work.

Anxious to read what it said, I opened it immediately after receiving it. I read that he was Mr. Sheppard, a well-known man of God and the pastor of Promise Land Ministries. I give this testimony because it is so important that you not judge a book by its cover because you will never know if you are entertaining a man or woman of God. It is written: "For whosoever shall be ashamed of me and of my words, of him shall the Son of man be ashamed, when he shall come in his own glory, and *in his*

Father's, and of the holy angels" (Luke 9:26). My thoughts were only to share the good news.

Eventually I had the pleasure of visiting his ministry and meeting his family and staff. God has really blessed me from this ministry. In the fall of 2007, Sister Noble and I were invited to their Seven Days of Glory celebration. A prophetic word was given over the audience on that night by the man of God that there would be "no more toiling" for the men and women of God. I received that word, and when the service ended, we had the pleasure of meeting the messenger of the evening, Dr. James Williams, and his lovely wife. And what was spoken—no more toiling—has come to pass in my life.

> Without faith it is impossible to please him: for he that cometh to God must believe that he is, and that he is a rewarder of them that diligently seek him. (Heb. 11:16)

The word of God will bring the revelation as the spirit of God through men and women who have a consecrated relationship with him. For example, he will give you the authority to speak as a prophet; not only will it bring prophetic inspiration, but confirmation. Once the evidence has presented itself, it has come to pass. But you must know that the prophetic word is for those who walk in faith as believers of Christ. Hallelujah! I am a witness to the prophetic word. It is written: "The natural man does not receive the things of the Spirit of God, for they are foolishness to him; nor can he know them, because they are spiritually discerned" (1 Cor. 2:14).

In the year 2008, Faith Works Church of God had grown, and we were ready for another building. God blessed us to move from the storefront to an actual church building, and our name changed from Faith Works to Greater Faith Works. Like any organization, you have your wave of members who come and go, yet we continued to press toward the mark of a higher calling with our Food and Clothes Ministry, Radio Ministry, and the annual DEAP (Drop Everything and Pray) Conference, keeping those in the community encouraged of the love that God has for us.

> the lord said unto the servant, Go out into the highways and hedges, and compel them to come in, that my house may be filled. (Luke 14:23)

May 27, 2008, was an unforgettable morning; I awakened with a song in my heart. It was so clear in my dream. I was standing in the middle of a circular auditorium singing the praises of Jesus and awakened singing a song I had never known. I immediately got the dictation recorder, and the words flowed from my mouth. I later played it back, only to say, "Thank you, Lord, for my birthday song." I was so excited that I shared it with a friend, and since that time, the Lord has blessed me with several other songs that I have yet to disclose as an aspiring songstress. That day meant more to me than just a song; it reassured me that I was alive through Christ. A void in my heart was filled with the joy only the Lord could give me. I was delivered from the circumstances in my life, giving me a new perspective. "I can do all things through Christ who strengthens me" (Phil. 4:13).

A pain-free life is a fantasy, and we don't live in a world of make-believe. On January 18, 2010, while at work, I got a phone call from my brother saying our mother had had multiple strokes and she was in CCU at the hospital. My first thought was to pray. As I prepared to make the trip, all I did was pray because I knew that God would answer my prayers. Upon arrival everyone was sitting patiently, waiting to see her. She stayed unresponsive for quite some time. She was only able to open her eyes, but I kept the faith, believing God was working. The bottom line was she is still here; therefore, in spite of my situation, God is good to me. She proceeded to come around once they changed her medication and started rehabilitation.

During her rehabilitation, on February 8 she lost her eldest sister. I was saddened to hear this, yet thankful that my mother was still living. The family was going through some changes, but God was with us. Unfortunately on May 12, another sibling passed, this time a brother, but God is still and always good. After the recessional of my uncle's funeral, my cousin Sharon from north Mississippi and I were conversing over the day's events. She introduced me to her pastor, the apostle, and his wife, who had come to the funeral too. Somehow the subject of prayer came about and my experiences of prayer that I had shared with Sharon. Before I knew it, their plans were to contact me at 5:00 a.m. as a prayer partner in the central Mississippi region.

Starting the very next day, May 20, I was up before sunrise to pray for our communities, the president, and those in leadership positions, as well as my mother, before going to work. This task, which ended January 2011, strengthened my pray life. I was amazed that God was transforming me. I have now developed a prayer life in the manner that God expects of me. And my mother is still among the living. Glory!

I have so many testimonies I can give on how God has made provision for each and every one

Commencement

of my needs and how he has blessed me through others. As the saints of old would say, I just can't tell it all. I want to give one more testimony.

In the summer of 2012, evening prayer was held at Greater faith works. After leaving the altar, Evangelist Warren asked me and two other young ladies to come back to the altar. She asked the pastor to anoint our heads with the oil and spoke these words: "God is going to use you through your writings." She then prayed over us. This was a confirmation that it was time.

As Aunt Joyce had reminded me during our last conversation, she felt I could help someone else who was going through the loss of a child. My journal was tucked away, one day to reveal to my children the story of their oldest sister, not only for them but for those nieces and nephews who knew of her existence, never to be seen again.

God had a plan for me. As I prayed about the direction I should go with this story, little by little he revealed things to me. I realized as I began to write of the occurrence of my life that the biggest conflict was within me, trying to fit in and being unfulfilled until I finally found my place through the word of God. I was instructed to write about my spiritual course. Like most, I was rebellious of the word of God, and I did things I thought were tolerable because the influences of the world made it seem to be all right. I was fooled by the devices of Satin, falling deeper into his snares, so that I too would be accompanying him in torment if my life had ended.

These experiences broke me. They molded me and made me over into the vessel of God that has testified of the things that he has brought me through. Once you know your place in Christ, the evildoers can no longer steal your joy because you know he has already defeated the enemy, for it is written in John 16:33 that Jesus said, "These things I have spoken unto you, that in me ye might have peace. In the world ye shall have tribulation: but be of good cheer; I have overcome the world." When the storms of life come your way, you have the covering of Christ to keep you, for it is written: "God hath not given us the spirit of fear; but of power, and of love, and of a sound mind" (2 Tim. 1:17).

I must share this with you: if he did it for me, he can do it for you. No matter what has happened in the past, you can commit your life to Christ. The only time it will be too late is if sudden death came upon you. Don't be confused. You cannot repent once your life is over. Therefore, I leave you with this: "Jesus answered and said unto them, Ye do err, not knowing the scriptures, nor the power of God" (Matt. 22:29). Get to know him, because he is truly all you need.

> A double minded man is unstable in all his ways. (James 1:18)

Let us pray.
Heavenly Father, I come to you broken. You know my needs, and you know my desires. Father, I understand that I must repent of my sins, and I must forgive those who despitefully use and abuse me. Father, I am asking you, as a believer of Christ who died for my sins and rose on the third day, with all power in his hands, that I may live life more abundantly through the riches of your word. Amen.

Thank you for allowing me to share with you the good news of Jesus Christ. I must confess that I have not spoken of Kenya's death in this manner until now. God has delivered me from the stronghold of grief and depression to let others know that they are not alone. If you want to know more about the word of God, search your community for a Bible-teaching church organization near you. May God bless you and keep you.

> Because thy loving-kindness is better than life, my lips shall praise thee. (Ps. 63:3)

Therefore, my beloved brethren, be ye steadfast, unmovable, always abounding in the work of the Lord, forasmuch as ye know that your labour is not in vain in the Lord.
1 Corinthians 15:58 (KJV)

Appendix

God has provided his people with the King James Bible, which gives the provisions needed to grow in grace as we strive to live in obedience to the teachings of Jesus Christ. Each day we are blessed with his love and mercy, showing he will never give up on us. I am thankful that he has given clear instructions through which I was able to find the love of Christ by seeking him diligently to understand just how much he cares about me. Below are the Scripture verses that made my acceptance of Jesus Christ a reality.

"And it shall come to pass in the last days, saith God, I will pour out of my Spirit upon all flesh: and your sons and your daughters shall prophesy, and your young men shall see visions, and your old men shall dream dreams" (Acts 2:17).

"The fear of the Lord is the beginning of knowledge: but fools despise wisdom and instruction" (Prov. 1:7).

"And wisdom and knowledge shall be the stability of thy times, and strength of salvation: the fear of the Lord is his treasure" (Isa. 33: 6).

"Casting all your care upon him; for he careth for you" (1 Peter 5:7).

"Be strong and of a good courage; be not afraid, neither be thou dismayed: for the Lord thy God is with thee whithersoever thou goest" (Josh. 1:9).

"Preserve me, O God: for in thee do I put my trust. My distress I cried unto the Lord, and he heard me" (Ps. 16:1).

"In my distress I cried unto the Lord, and he heard me" (Ps. 120:1).

"For whatsoever things were written aforetime were written for our learning, that we through patience and comfort of the scriptures might have hope" (Rom. 15:4).

"I Will lift up mine eyes unto the hills, from whence cometh my help" (Ps. 121:1).

"And Jesus called a little child unto him, and set him in the midst of them ... And said, Verily I say unto you, Except ye be converted, and become as little children, ye shall not enter into the kingdom of heaven" (Matt. 18:2, 4).

"And we know that all things work together for good to them that love God, to them who are the called according to his purpose" (Rom. 8:28).

"Study to shew thyself approved unto God, a workman that needeth not to be ashamed, rightly dividing the word of truth" (2 Tim. 2:15).

"Before I formed thee in the belly I knew thee; and before thou camest forth out of the womb I sanctified thee, and I ordained thee a prophet unto the nations" (Jer. 1:5).

"Then Peter said unto them, Repent, and be baptized every one of you in the name of Jesus Christ for the remission of sins, and ye shall receive the gift of the Holy Ghost" (Acts 2:38).

"And be not conformed to this world: but be ye transformed by the renewing of your mind, that ye may prove what is that good, and acceptable, and perfect, will of God" (Rom. 12: 2).

"Train up a child in the way he should go: and when he is old, he will not depart from it" (Prov. 22:6).

"He that covereth his sins shall not prosper: but whoso confesseth and forsaketh them shall have mercy" (Prov. 28:3).

"Come unto me, all ye that labour and are heavy laden, and I will give you rest. Take my yoke upon you, and learn of me; for I am meek and lowly in heart: and ye shall find rest unto your souls. For my yoke is easy, and my burden is light" (Matt. 11:28–30).

"Enter ye in at the strait gate: for wide is the gate, and broad is the way, that leadeth to destruction, and many there be which go in thereafter: Because strait is the gate, and narrow is the way, which leadeth unto life, and few there be that find it" (Matt. 7:13–14).

"Jesus Christ the same yesterday, and today, and forever" (Heb. 13:8).

"But seek ye first the kingdom of God, and his righteousness; and all these things shall be added unto you" (Matt. 6:33).

"Not forsaking the assembling of ourselves together, as the manner of some is; but exhorting one another: and so much the more, as ye see the day approaching" (Heb. 10:25).

"For my thoughts are not your thoughts, neither are your ways my ways, saith the Lord" (Isa. 55:8).

"For I know the thoughts that I think toward you, saith the Lord, thoughts of peace, and not of evil, to give you an expected end" (Jer. 29:11).

"Open thou mine eyes, that I may behold wondrous things out of thy law" (Ps. 119: 18).

"And it came to pass, that, while Apollos was at Corinth, Paul having passed through the upper coasts came to Ephesus: and finding certain disciples, He said unto them, Have ye received the Holy Ghost since ye believed? And they said unto him, We have not so much as heard whether there be any Holy Ghost. And he said unto them, Unto what then were ye baptized? And they said, Unto John's baptism. Then said Paul, John verily baptized with the baptism of repentance, saying unto the people, that they should believe on him which should come after him, that is, on Christ Jesus. When they heard this, they were baptized in the name of the Lord Jesus. And when Paul had laid his hands upon them, the Holy Ghost came on them; and they spake with tongues, and prophesied. And all the men were about twelve" (Acts 19:1–7).

"But ye are not in the flesh, but in the Spirit, if so be that the Spirit of God dwell in you. Now if any man have not the Spirit of Christ, he is none of his" (Rom. 8:9).

"The fear of man bringeth a snare: but whoso putteth his trust in the Lord shall be safe" (Prov. 29:25).

"Not everyone that saith unto me, Lord, Lord, shall enter into the kingdom of heaven; but he that doeth the will of my Father which is in heaven" (Matt. 7:21).

"For whosoever shall be ashamed of me and of my words, of him shall the Son of man be ashamed, when he shall come in his own glory, and in his Father's, and of the holy angels" (Luke 9:26).

"But without faith it is impossible to please him: for he that cometh to God must believe that he is, and that he is a rewarder of them that diligently seek him" (Heb. 11:6).

"To open their eyes, and to turn them from darkness to light, and from the power of Satan unto God, that they may receive forgiveness of sins, and inheritance among them which are sanctified by faith that is in me" (Acts 26:18).

"But the natural man receiveth not the things of the Spirit of God: for they are foolishness unto him: neither can he know them, because they are spiritually discerned" (1 Cor. 2:14).

"And the lord said unto the servant, Go out into the highways and hedges, and compel them to come in, that my house may be filled" (Luke 14:23).

"I can do all things through Christ which strengthen me" (Phil. 4:13).

"A double minded man is unstable in all his ways" (James 1:48).

"Because thy loving-kindness is better than life, my lips shall praise thee" (Ps. 63:3).

"In everything give thanks for this is the will of God in Christ Jesus concerning you" (1 Thess. 5:8).

Notes

Notes

Notes

Notes

CPSIA information can be obtained at www.ICGtesting.com
Printed in the USA
LVOW11s0326251115

464139LV00001B/25/P